PENGUIN MODERN EUROPEAN POETS

D91

FOUR GREEK POETS

C. P. CAVAFY · GEORGE SEFERIS

ODYSSEUS ELYTIS · NIKOS GATSOS

FOUR GREEK POETS

C. P. CAVAFY

GEORGE SEFERIS

ODYSSEUS ELYTIS

NIKOS GATSOS

*Poems chosen and translated from
the Greek by Edmund Keeley
and Philip Sherrard*

Penguin Books

Penguin Books Ltd, Harmondsworth, Middlesex, England
Penguin Books Pty Ltd, Ringwood, Victoria, Australia

—

This selection first published 1966

—

Copyright © Penguin Books, 1966

—

Made and printed in Great Britain
by Cox & Wyman Ltd,
London, Fakenham, and Reading
Set in Monotype Garamond

Contents

CONTENTS

*Notes are provided on pages 106–10 in explanation of the words or lines marked with superior numbers in the ensuing poems.

Acknowledgements

For permission to reproduce certain of
the translations in this book acknow-
ledgement is made to Thames and
Hudson Ltd. We are also grateful for the
cooperation of Mr Odysseus Elytis, Mr
Nikos Gatsos, Mr George Seferis, and
Mr Alexander Singopoulos.

The translations of Cavafy are pub-
lished by permission of The Hogarth
Press, who publish THE COMPLETE
POEMS OF C. P. CAVAFY, translated by
Rae Dalven.

C. P. CAVAFY

Waiting for the Barbarians

What are we waiting for, gathered in the market-place?

    The barbarians are to arrive today.

Why so little activity in the senate?
Why do the senators sit there without legislating?

    Because the barbarians will arrive today.
    What laws should the senators make now?
    The barbarians, when they come, will do the legislating.

Why has our emperor risen so early,
and why does he sit at the largest gate of the city
on the throne, in state, wearing the crown?

    Because the barbarians will arrive today.
    And the emperor is waiting to receive
    their leader. He has even prepared
    a parchment for him. There
    he has given him many titles and names.

Why did our two consuls and our praetors go out
today in the scarlet, the embroidered, togas?
Why did they wear bracelets with so many amethysts,
and rings with brilliant sparkling emeralds?
Why today do they carry precious staves
splendidly inlaid with silver and gold?

    Because the barbarians will arrive today;
    and such things dazzle barbarians.

And why don't the worthy orators come as always
to make their speeches, say what they have to say?

Because the barbarians will arrive today;
and they are bored by eloquence and public speaking.

What does this sudden uneasiness mean,
and this confusion? (How grave the faces have become!)
Why are the streets and squares rapidly emptying,
and why is everyone going back home so lost in thought?

Because it is night and the barbarians have not come.
And some men have arrived from the frontiers
and they say that barbarians don't exist any longer.

And now, what will become of us without barbarians?
They were a kind of solution.

The City

You said: 'I'll go to another land, go to another sea,
find some other town better than this one.
Fated, condemned, is all that I've ever done
and my heart, like a dead body, is buried in a tomb.
How long must my mind remain within this gloom?
When I cast my eyes about me, look no matter where,
I see the black ruins of my life, here,
where I've spent so many years – wasted them, destroyed them
    utterly.'

You will not find new lands, not find another sea.
The city will follow you. You'll wander down
these very streets, age in these same quarters of the town,
among the same houses finally turn grey.
You'll reach this city always. Don't hope to get away:
for you there is no ship, no road anywhere.
As you've destroyed your life here,
in this small corner, so in the whole world you've wrecked it
    utterly.

The God Abandons Antony[1]

When suddenly at midnight you hear
an invisible company pass
with exquisite music, voices –
do not lament your luck that now gives out, your work
that has failed, schemes of your life
all proved to be false – do not lament these uselessly.
Like one for long prepared, like a courageous man,
say good-bye to her, to the Alexandria who is leaving.
Above all, do not deceive yourself, do not say
it was a dream, your hearing was mistaken:
do not condescend to such vain hopes as these.
Like one for long prepared, like a courageous man,
as it becomes you who have had the honour of such a city,
go firmly to the window
and listen, with feeling but not
with a coward's supplication and complaint –
listen as the final enjoyment to the music,
to the exquisite instruments of the mysterious company,
and say good-bye to her, to the Alexandria you are losing.

Ithaka

When you set out for Ithaka
ask that your way be long,
full of adventure, full of instruction.
The Laistrygonians and the Cyclops,
angry Poseidon – do not fear them:
such as these you will never find
as long as your thought is lofty, as long as a rare
emotion touch your spirit and your body.
The Laistrygonians and the Cyclops,
angry Poseidon – you will not meet them
unless you carry them in your soul,
unless your soul raise them up before you.

Ask that your way be long.
At many a summer dawn to enter
– with what gratitude, what joy –
ports seen for the first time;
to stop at Phoenician trading centres,
and to buy good merchandise,
mother of pearl and coral, amber and ebony,
and sensuous perfumes of every kind,
sensuous perfumes as lavishly as you can;
to visit many Egyptian cities,
to gather stores of knowledge from the learnèd.

Have Ithaka always in your mind.
Your arrival there is what you are destined for.
But don't in the least hurry the journey.
Better it last for years,
so that when you reach the island you are old,
rich with all you have gained on the way,
not expecting Ithaka to give you wealth.

Ithaka gave you the splendid journey.
Without her you would not have set out.
She hasn't anything else to give you.

And if you find her poor, Ithaka hasn't deceived you.
So wise have you become, of such experience,
that already you'll have understood what these Ithakas
mean.

Philhellene[2]

Be sure the engraving is done artistically.
The expression grave and dignified.
The crown preferably narrow:
I don't care for the broad Parthian type.
The inscription, as usual, in Greek:
not exaggerated, not pompous –
one doesn't want it misunderstood by the proconsul
who's always nosing things out and reporting to Rome –
yet of course honorific.
Something most choice on the other side:
some discus-thrower, young, beautiful.
Above all I recommend you see to it
(Sithaspes, in God's name, don't let it be forgotten)
that after the King and the Saviour
there be engraved in elegant characters: Philhellene.
And now don't start your facetiousness,
your 'Where are the Greeks?' and 'What hellenism
here behind Zagros, out beyond Phraata?'
Since so many others more barbarian than ourselves
inscribe it, we shall inscribe it too.
And, moreover, don't forget that sometimes
sophists come to us from Syria,
and versifiers, and other such triflers.
Thus we are not, I trust, un-hellenic.

Theodotus

If you are among the truly select,
watch how you obtain your dominance.
However greatly you are glorified, however much
the states proclaim your achievements
in Italy and in Thessaly,
whatever honours
your admirers in Rome decree for you,
neither your joy, nor the triumph will remain,
nor superior – superior indeed! – will you feel,
when, in Alexandria, Theodotus brings you
upon a blood-stained platter
the wretched Pompey's head.[3]

And do not be certain that in your life
restricted, regulated, and prosaic,
such spectacular and dreadful things do not take place.
Perhaps at this moment into some neighbour's
well-ordered house there goes –
invisible, unsubstantial – Theodotus,
bringing exactly such a frightful head.

Manuel Comnenos[4]

The Emperor Manuel Comnenos
one sad September day
felt himself close to death. The astrologers
(salaried) of the court insisted
that he still had many more years to live.
While, however, they were talking, he
remembers ancient pious custom,
and from the monastic cells he orders
ecclesiastical vestments to be brought,
and he wears them, and is glad that he shows
the modest aspect of a priest or a monk.

Fortunate all those who believe,
and like the Emperor Manuel end their lives
clothed so modestly according to their faith.

One of Their Gods

When one of them passed through the market
of Seleukeia, at about the hour of dusk,
like a tall youth of perfect beauty,
with the joy of the inviolate in his eyes,
with his black and perfumed hair,
the passers-by would gaze at him,
and one would ask the other if he knew him,
and if he were a Greek from Syria, or a stranger.
But some who looked with greater care
would understand and move to one side;
and while he was lost beneath the colonnade,
among the shadows and the lights of evening,
going towards the quarter that lives
only at night, with orgies and debauchery,
with every kind of drunkenness and lust,
they would wonder which of Them it could be,
and for what suspicious pleasure
he had come down into the streets of Seleukeia
from the Venerated, Most-Honoured Mansions.

The Respite of Nero

He wasn't worried, Nero, when he heard
the pronouncement of the Delphic Oracle:
'Beware the seventy-third year.'
Time still to rejoice.
He is thirty. Ample indeed
the period the god bestows
for him to deal with future dangers.

Now, a little tired, he will return to Rome
but splendidly tired after that journey
which was all days of enjoyment –
theatres, garden-parties, gymnasiums. . . .
Evenings in the cities of Achaia. . . .
Ah, the delight above all of naked bodies. . . .

So Nero. And in Spain Galba
secretly gathers his army and drills it –
Galba, the old man in his seventy-third year.[5]

Of Demetrius Soter (162-150 B.C.) [6]

His every expectation turned out wrong!

He had imagined performing famous deeds,
to end the humiliation that since the battle
of Magnesia had oppressed his fatherland,
to make Syria again a powerful state,
with her armies, her fleets,
her big fortresses, her wealth.

He suffered, he became bitter at Rome
when he felt in the conversations of his friends,
the youth of the great families,
with all the delicacy and politeness
that they showed to him, to the son
of King Seleukos Philopater –
when he felt that none the less there was always
a secret contempt for the hellenizing dynasties:
that they are fallen, are not fit for anything serious,
quite unsuited for the leadership of peoples.
He drew apart, and he became indignant, and he swore
that it would not be at all as they imagined;
why, he has will-power;
he will struggle, he will achieve, he will exalt.
If only he could find a way of getting to the East,
succeed in escaping from Italy –
and all this strength he has
within his soul, all this energy
he will communicate to the people.

Ah, only to find himself in Syria!
So young he left his country
he scarcely remembers her appearance.

But in his thoughts he has conceived her always
as something holy to be approached with reverence,
as the sight of a lovely place, as the vision
of Greek cities and Greek ports.

And now?
    Now desperation and sorrow.

They were right, the young men in Rome.
It is not possible for them to endure, the dynasties
resulting from the Occupation of the Macedonians.

No matter: he himself has striven,
he has struggled as much as he could.
And in his black disillusion
one thing only he prides himself on still:
that, even in his failure,
he presents to the world the same indomitable courage.

The rest: they were dreams and vanities.
This Syria: it almost does not seem to be his country;
this Syria is the land of Heracleides and of Balas.

Darius

The poet Phernazis is composing
the important part of his epic poem:
how Darius, son of Hystaspes,
took over the kingdom of the Persians. (From him
descends our glorious king,
Mithridates, Dionysus and Eupator.)[7] But here
philosophy is needed: he has to analyse
the feelings Darius must have had:
arrogance perhaps and intoxication? But no – more likely
a certain understanding of the vanity of greatness.
Deeply the poet ponders the matter.

But his servant, running in,
interrupts him and announces most significant news.
The war with the Romans has begun.
Most of our army has crossed the borders.

The poet is dumbfounded. What a calamity!
How can our glorious king,
Mithridates, Dionysus and Eupator,
concern himself now with Greek poems!
In the middle of a war – imagine, Greek poems!

Phernazis frets. What bad luck!
Just when he was certain with his 'Darius'
to distinguish himself, and to confound
once and for all his envious critics.
What a postponement, what a postponement of his plans.

And if it were only a postponement – good enough.
But let us see whether we are safe
in Amisus. It is not a city fortified exceptionally well.
The Romans are the most frightful enemies.

Are we, the Cappadocians, able to cope
with them? Could it be possible?
Are we to measure ourselves with the legions?
Great gods, protectors of Asia, help us.

But in all his agitation and misfortune
insistently the poetical idea comes and goes –
the most likely of course is arrogance and intoxication:
arrogance and intoxication must Darius have felt.

An Exiled Byzantine Nobleman Versifying

Let the frivolous call me frivolous.
To serious matters I was always
most attentive. And I will insist
that no one knows better than myself
the Holy Fathers or the Scriptures, or the Canons of the
  Synods.
In every one of his doubts, in every
ecclesiastical difficulty, Botaneiatis
consulted me, me first of all.
But exiled here (let her beware, the malicious
Irene Doukaina),[8] and incredibly bored,
it is not altogether out of place to amuse myself
making six-line and eight-line verses –
to amuse myself with the mythology
of Hermes and Apollo and Dionysus,
or the heroes of Thessaly and the Peloponnese;
and to compose correct iambics,
such as – if you will allow me to say so – the learnèd
at Constantinople do not know how to compose.
This correctness is, probably, the cause of their reproach.

From the School of the Renowned Philosopher

For two years he was a pupil of Ammonius Sakkas;[9]
but he was bored by both the philosophy and Sakkas.

After that he went into politics.
But he gave them up. The Prefect was a fool,
and his entourage officious and solemn blockheads:
their Greek disgusting, the idiots.

His curiosity was attracted
a little by the Church: to be baptized
and to pass as a Christian. But quickly
he changed his mind. He would quarrel no doubt
with his parents, ostentatious pagans;
and they at once would stop – a frightful thing –
their most generous allowance.

He had however to do something. He began to haunt
the corrupt houses of Alexandria,
every secret den of debauchery.

Fortune had been kind to him in this:
she had given him an extremely handsome figure.
And he enjoyed the divine gift.

At least for ten years yet
would his beauty last. Afterwards –
perhaps he will go again to Sakkas.
Or if in the meantime the old man has died,
he will go to another philosopher or sophist:
someone suitable is always to be found.

Or in the end possibly he will return
even to politics – laudably remembering
the traditions of his family,
duty towards the country, and other similar pomposities.

Julian and the Antiochians[10]

'Neither the letter CHI, they say, nor the letter KAPPA had ever harmed the city. . . . We, finding interpreters . . . were taught that these are the initial letters of names, the first of "Christ" and the second of "Konstantios".'

Julian's *Misopogon* (The Beard-hater).

Was it ever possible for them to renounce
their beautiful way of life; the variety
of their habitual amusements; the brilliance
of their theatre which consummated a union between Art
and the erotic tendencies of the flesh!

Immoral to a degree – and probably to more than a degree –
they were. But they had the satisfaction that their life
was the much talked of life of Antioch,
the delectable, the absolutely elegant.

To give up all this in order to attend, indeed, to what?

To his vapourings about the false gods;
his tedious self-advertisement;
his childish fear of the theatre;
his graceless prudery; his ludicrous beard.

O certainly they preferred the CHI,
certainly they preferred the KAPPA – a hundred times.

A Great Procession of Priests and Laymen

A procession of priests and laymen,
each walk of life represented,
passes through streets, through squares, and through gates
of the famous city of Antioch.
At the head of the great imposing procession
a beautiful white-clad youth is holding
with upraised hands the Cross,
our strength and our hope, the holy Cross.
The pagans, before so thoroughly arrogant,
but submissive now, and cowards, quickly
move away from the procession.
Far from us, far from us let them remain for ever
(as long as they do not renounce their error). The holy Cross
goes forward. Into every quarter
where Christians live with reverence for God
it brings consolation and joy:
and the pious come to the doors of their houses
and full of exultation they worship it –
the strength, the salvation of the universe, the Cross.

This is an annual Christian festival.
But today, observe, it takes place more splendidly.
The empire is delivered at last.
The most depraved, the appalling
Julian reigns no longer.

For the most pious Jovian let our prayers be given.[11]

In a Large Greek Colony, 200 B.C.

That things in the Colony do not proceed as they should
no one can doubt any longer,
and although in spite of everything we do go forward,
perhaps, as not a few are thinking, the time has come
to introduce a Political Reformer.

But the objection and the difficulty is
that they make an enormous fuss
about everything, these
reformers. (It would be a blessing
if they were never needed.) Whatever it is,
even the smallest detail, they question and investigate,
and at once radical reforms enter their heads
demanding to be executed without delay.

Also they have a liking for sacrifice:
RID YOURSELF OF THAT POSSESSION;
YOUR OWNERSHIP IS DANGEROUS:
EXACTLY SUCH POSSESSIONS DAMAGE COLONIES.
RID YOURSELF OF THAT INCOME,
AND OF THE OTHER CONNECTED WITH IT,
AND OF THIS THIRD, AS A NATURAL CONSEQUENCE;
THEY ARE ESSENTIAL, BUT WHAT CAN ONE DO?
THEY CREATE AN INJURIOUS RESPONSIBILITY FOR YOU.

And as they extend their investigation
they discover endless superfluities, and these they seek to re-
    move:
things which are however renounced with difficulty.

And when, with luck, the business is completed,
and every detail is defined and circumscribed,
they retire, taking also the wages due to them,

allowing us to see whatever still remains, after
such effective surgery.

Perhaps the moment has not yet arrived.
Let us not hurry: speed is a dangerous thing.
Untimely measures bring repentance.
Certainly, and unhappily, many things are wrong in the
    Colony.
But is there anything human without imperfection?
And after all, look, we do go forward.

In Sparta [12]

He did not know, the king Kleomenes, he did not dare –
he did not know how to tell his mother
of such a condition: that Ptolemy had demanded,
to guarantee their treaty, that she be sent
to Egypt and that she be held there:
a very humiliating, improper thing.
And every time he was about to tell her, he hesitated.
And every time he began to speak, he stopped.

But the wonderful woman understood him
(she had heard rumours already concerning it),
and she encouraged him to explain.
And she laughed; and she said of course she would go.
And she even rejoiced that she was able
in her old age to be useful to Sparta still.

As for the humiliation – it did not interest her.
The spirit of Sparta certainly was beyond
the comprehension of an upstart like the Lagides;
therefore his demand could not in fact
humiliate an Illustrious Woman like herself:
mother of a Spartan king.

Myris: Alexandria, A.D. 340

When I learnt of the tragedy, that Myris was dead,
I went to his house, although I avoid
going into the houses of Christians,
especially at times of mourning or festivity.

I stood in the corridor. I did not wish
to go further inside, because I perceived
that the relatives of the dead regarded me
with evident surprise and displeasure.

They had him in a large room
of which from the corner where I stood
I could see a little: all precious carpets,
and vessels of silver and gold.

I stood and wept in a corner of the corridor.
And I thought how our gatherings and our excursions
wouldn't be worthwhile any longer without Myris;
and I thought how I would no longer see him
at our beautiful and indecent all-night sessions
enjoying himself, and laughing, and reciting verses
with his perfect feel for Greek rhythm;
and I thought how I'd lost for ever
his beauty, how I'd lost for ever
the young man I'd worshipped so madly.

Some old women, close to me, were speaking softly
of the last day that he lived –
on his lips continually the name of Christ,
in his hand a cross.
And then four Christian priests
came into the room, and said prayers
fervently, and orisons to Jesus,
or to Mary (I do not know their religion well).

We had known, of course, that Myris was a Christian.
From the first moment we had known it, when
the year before last he'd joined our company.
But he lived exactly as we did:
more given to pleasure than all of us,
he scattered his money lavishly on amusements.
Indifferent to the world's esteem,
he threw himself eagerly into the nocturnal fights
when our band happened to meet
a rival band.
He never spoke of his religion.
And once we even told him
that we would take him with us to the Serapion.
But it was as if it displeased him,
this joke of ours: I remember now.
Ah, and now I recall two other occasions.
When we made libations to Poseidon,
he drew himself back from our circle and looked elsewhere.
When one of us enthusiastically said:
'Let our company be under
the favour and the protection of the great,
of the all-beautiful Apollo' – Myris whispered
(the others didn't hear) 'with the exception of myself'.

The Christian priests with loud voices
were praying for the young man's soul.
I noticed with how much diligence
and with what intensive care
for the forms of their religion, they were preparing
everything for the Christian funeral.
And suddenly an odd sensation
came to me. I felt obscurely
as if Myris were going from me:
I felt that he, a Christian, had united

with his own people, and that I was becoming
a stranger , a complete stranger; I even felt
a doubt approaching: that I'd been deceived
by my passion, and had always been a stranger to him.
I threw myself out of their frightful house,
I fled quickly before it was seized, before it was altered
by their Christianity, the memory of Myris.

To Have Taken the Trouble

I'm almost a vagabond and penniless.
This fatal city, Antioch,
has devoured all my money:
this fatal city with its extravagant life.

But I'm young and in excellent health.
A prodigious master of Greek,
I know Aristotle and Plato through and through,
as well as whatever orator, poet, or other author you may
    mention.
Of military affairs I am not ignorant,
and I have friends among the senior regular officers.
I have a certain knowledge also of administrative matters.
I spent six months in Alexandria last year;
something I know (and this is useful) about what goes on
    there:
the corruption, and the dirt, and the rest of it.

So I believe I am completely
qualified to serve this country,
my beloved fatherland, Syria.

In whatever job they put me I shall endeavour
to be useful to the country. That is my purpose.
But again, if they hinder me with their systems –
we know them, these smart ones: need we speak of it now? –
if they hinder me it's not my fault.

I will address myself to Zabinas first,
and if that idiot doesn't appreciate me,
I shall go to his rival, Grypos.
And if that imbecile doesn't appoint me,
I shall go at once to Hyrcanus.[13]

In any case one of the three will want me.

And my conscience is quiet
about my indifference to the choice:
the three of them damage Syria to the same extent.

But, a ruined man, it's not my fault.
I'm only trying, poor devil, to make ends meet.
The almighty gods ought to have taken the trouble
to create a fourth, an honest man.
Gladly I'd have gone along with him.

In the Outskirts of Antioch [14]

We were astonished in Antioch when we heard
about the new activities of Julian.

Apollo explained things to him, at Daphne!
He did not wish to give an oracle (as though we cared!),
he did not intend to speak prophetically, unless first
his temple at Daphne were cleansed.
The neighbouring dead, he declared, annoyed him.

Many tombs are to be found at Daphne.
One of those there buried
was the wonderful, holy, and triumphant
martyr Babylas, the glory of our church.

It was him the false god hinted at, him he feared.
As long as he felt him close he did not dare
to give his oracle: not a whisper.
(The false gods are terrified of our martyrs).

The unholy Julian rolled up his sleeves,
became angry and shouted: 'Raise him, carry him out,
take him away immediately, this Babylas.
Do you hear there? Apollo is annoyed.
Raise him, seize him at once,
dig him out, dispose of him where you like.
Take him away, expel him. Is this a game?
Apollo said the temple is to be cleansed'.

We took it, we carried it, the holy relic, elsewhere.
We took it, we carried it, in love and in honour.

And excellently indeed has the temple prospered!
No time had elapsed when a colossal fire
flared up; a terrible fire;
and both the temple and Apollo were burnt.

Ashes the idol; sweepings, with the rubbish.

Julian exploded, and he spread it round –
what else could he do? – that we, the Christians,
had set the fire. Let him say so.
It hasn't been proved. Let him say so.
The essential thing is – that he exploded.

GEORGE SEFERIS

From *Mythical Story* [15]

I

For three years
we waited intently for the messenger
watching closely
the pines the shore and the stars.
One with the plough's blade or the keel of the ship,
we were searching to find the first seed
that the ancient drama might begin again.

We returned to our homes broken,
our limbs incapable, our mouths ruined
by the taste of rust and brine.
When we awoke we journeyed towards the north, strangers
plunged into mists by the spotless wings of swans that woun-
    ded us.
On winter nights the strong wind from the east maddened us,
in the summers we were lost in the agony of the day which
    could not die.

We brought back
these carved reliefs of a humble art.

From *Mythical Story*

3

'Remember the bath by which you were slain'
Aeschylus, *The Libation Bearers*, 491.

I awoke with this marble head in my hands
which exhausts my elbows and I do not know where to set it
    down.
It was falling into the dream as I was coming out of the dream
so our lives joined and it will be very difficult to part them.

I look at the eyes: neither open nor closed
I speak to the mouth which keeps trying to speak
I hold the cheeks which have passed beyond the skin
I have no more strength.

My hands disappear and come back to me
mutilated.

From *Mythical Story*

4
ARGONAUTS

And the soul,
if she is to know herself,
must look
into the soul:[16]
the stranger and enemy, we saw him in the mirror.

The companions were good lads: they did not complain
either at the labour or the thirst or the frost,
they had the bearing of trees and waves
which accept the wind and the rain
accept the night and the sun
without changing in the midst of change.
They were good lads, whole days
they sweated at the oar with lowered eyes
breathing in rhythm
and their blood reddened a submissive skin.
Sometimes they sang, with lowered eyes
when we passed the desolate island with the barbary figs
to the west, beyond the cape of the dogs
that bark.

If she is to know herself, they said
into the soul she must look, they said
and the oars struck the gold of the sea
in the sunset.
We passed many capes many islands the sea
leading to the other sea, gulls and seals.
Sometimes unfortunate women wept
lamenting their lost children

and others raging sought Alexander the Great
and glories buried in the depths of Asia.
We moored on shores full of night-scents
with the singing of birds, waters which left on the hands
the memory of a great happiness.
But the voyages did not end.
Their souls became one with the oars and the rowlocks
with the solemn face of the prow
with the channel made by the rudder
with the water that shattered their image.
The companions with lowered eyes
died one by one. Their oars
mark the place where they sleep by the shore.[17]

No one remembers them. Justice.

From *Mythical Story*

5

We did not know them –
              it was hope deep down that said
we had known them since early childhood.
We saw them perhaps twice and then they took to the ships;
cargoes of coal, cargoes of grain, and our friends
lost beyond the ocean forever.
Dawn finds us beside the weary lamp
drawing on the paper, with great effort and awkwardly,
ships, mermaids or sea-shells;
at dusk we go down to the river
because it shows us the way to the sea;
and we spend the nights in cellars that smell of tar.

Our friends have left us
              perhaps we never saw them, perhaps
we met them when sleep
still brought us close to the breathing wave
perhaps we seek them because we seek the other life
beyond the statues.

From *Mythical Story*

8

What do our souls seek journeying
on the decks of decayed ships
crowded with sallow women and crying infants
unable to forget themselves, either with the flying fish
or with the stars which the tips of the masts indicate,
grated by gramophone records
bound unwillingly by non-existent pilgrimages
murmuring broken thoughts from foreign tongues?

What do our souls seek journeying
on rotten, sea-borne timbers
from harbour to harbour?
Shifting broken stones, inhaling
the pine's coolness with less ease each day
swimming in the waters of this sea
and of that sea
without touch
without men
in a country which is no longer ours
nor yours.

We knew that the islands were beautiful
somewhere round about here where we are groping –
a little lower or a little higher,
the slightest distance.

From *Mythical Story*

9

The harbour is old, I cannot wait any longer
for the friend who left for the island of pine-trees
or the friend who left for the island of plane-trees
or the friend who left for the open sea.
I caress the rusted cannons, I caress the oars
so that my body may revive and become resolute.
The sails give off the odour only
of salt from the other storm.

If I wanted to remain alone, what I sought
was solitude, not such expectation
the shattering of my soul at the horizon
these lines, these colours, this silence.

The stars of the night bring me back to the anticipation
of Odysseus awaiting the dead among the asphodels.[18]
When we moored here among the asphodels we wished to find
the gorge which knew Adonis wounded.

From *Mythical Story*

10

Our country is enclosed, all mountains
which have the low sky for a roof day and night.
We have no rivers, we have no wells, we have no springs,
only a few cisterns – and these empty – which echo and which
  we worship.
A sound stagnant, hollow, the same as our loneliness
the same as our love, the same as our bodies.
We find it strange that once we were able to build
our houses, huts, and sheepfolds.
And our marriages, the cool coronals and the fingers
become enigmas inexplicable to our soul.
How were our children born, how did they grow?

Our country is enclosed. The two black
Symplegades[19] enclose it. When we go down
to the harbours on Sunday to breathe
we see, alight in the sunset,
the broken timbers of voyages unfinished
bodies that no longer know how to love.

From *Mythical Story*

12

BOTTLE IN THE SEA

Three rocks, a few burnt pines, an abandoned chapel
and farther above
the same landscape repeated starts again;
three rocks in the shape of a gate-way, rusted,
a few burnt pines, black and yellow,
and a square hut buried in whitewash;
and farther above, the same landscape
recurs level after level
to the horizon, to the darkening sky.

Here we moored the ship to splice the broken oars
to drink water and to sleep.
The sea which embittered us is deep and unexplored
and unfolds a boundless calm.
Here among the pebbles we found a coin
and threw dice for it.
The youngest won it and disappeared.[20]

We set out again with our broken oars.

From *Mythical Story*

15

'Quid πλατανῶν opacissimus?' Pliny, *Letters*, 1, 3.

Sleep enfolded you in green leaves like a tree
you breathed like a tree in the quiet light
in the translucent spring I watched your form:
eyelids closed, eyelashes brushing the water.
In the soft grass my fingers found your fingers
I held your pulse a moment
and felt elsewhere your heart's pain.

Beneath the plane-tree, near the water, amidst the laurel
sleep removed you and scattered you
around me, near me, without my being able to touch the whole
    of you
one as you were with your silence;
seeing your shadow grow and diminish,
lose itself in the other shadows, in the other
world which released you yet held you back.

The life which they gave us to live, we lived.
Pity those who wait with such patience
lost in the black laurel beneath the heavy plane-trees
and those who speak in solitude to cisterns and wells
and drown in the voice's circles.
Pity the companion who shared our privations and our sweat,
who plunged into the sun like a crow beyond the ruins
without hope of enjoying our reward.

Give us, beyond sleep, serenity.

From *Mythical Story*

22

So very much having passed before our eyes
that our eyes in the end saw nothing but, beyond
and behind, memory like the white drape one night in an en-
  closure
where we saw strange visions, even stranger than you,
pass by and vanish in the motionless foliage of a pepper-tree;

Having known this fate of ours so well
wandering around among broken stones, three or six thousand
  years
searching in collapsed buildings which might have been our
  homes
trying to remember dates and heroic deeds:
shall we now be able?

Having been bound and scattered,
having struggled, as they said, with non-existent difficulties
lost, finding again a road full of blind regiments
sinking in marshes and in the lake of Marathon,
shall we now be able to die properly?

From *Mythical Story*

24

Here end the works of the sea, the works of love.
Those who will some day live here where we end –
if the blood should chance to darken in their memory and
  overflow –
let them not forget us, the weak souls among the asphodels,[21]
let them turn towards Erebus the heads of the victims:[22]

We who had nothing will teach them peace.

Santorini[23]

Stoop if you can to the dark sea forgetting
the flute's sound on naked feet
that trod your sleep in the other, the sunken life.

Write if you can on your last shell
the day, the name, the place,
and fling it into the sea so that it sinks.

We found ourselves naked on the pumice-stone
watching the rising islands,
watching the red islands go down
into their sleep, into our sleep.
Here we found ourselves naked, holding
the scales weighted on the side of injustice.

Instep of power, unshadowed will, calculated love,
projects that ripen in the mid-day sun,
course of fate with the beat of a young hand
on the shoulder;
in this land that is scattered, that cannot resist,
in this land that was once our land,
the islands – rust and ashes – are sinking.

Altars destroyed
and friends forgotten:
leaves of the palmtree in mud.

Let your hands, if you can, go journeying
here on the curve of time with that ship
which has touched the horizon.
When the dice have struck the slate,
when the lance has struck the breast-plate,

when the eye has recognized the stranger,
and love has dried up
in punctured souls;
when looking round you see
everywhere the feet harvested,
everywhere the hands dead,
everywhere the eyes darkened;
when you can't even choose any longer
the death you would like to be yours,
hearing a cry,
even the wolf's cry,
your due:
let your hands, if you can, go journeying,
free yourself from the faithless time,
and sink
as sinks whoever raises the great stones.

The King of Asine

’Ασίνην τε . .

Iliad, II, 560

We looked all morning round the citadel[24]
starting from the shaded side, there where the sea,
green and without reflection – breast of a slain peacock –
accepted us like time without a single gap.
The veins of rock descended from high above,
twisted vines, naked, many-branched, coming alive
at the touch of water, while the eye following them
fought to escape the tiresome rocking,
losing strength continually.

On the sunny side, a long open beach
and the light striking diamonds on the large walls.
No living thing, the wild doves gone
and the King of Asine, whom we have been searching for two
   years now,
unknown, forgotten by all, even by Homer,
only one word in the *Iliad* and that uncertain,
thrown there like the gold burial mask.
You touched it, remember its sound? Hollow in the light
like a dry jar in dug earth:
the same sound that our oars make in the sea.
The King of Asine a void beneath the mask
everywhere with us everywhere with us, behind a single
   phrase:
‘‘Ασίνην τε . . . ’Ασίνην τε . . .’
      and his children statues
and his desires the fluttering of birds, and the wind
in the interstices of his thoughts, and his ships
anchored in a vanished port:
beneath the mask a void.

Behind the large eyes the curved lips the curls
in relief on the gold cover of our being
a dark spot which you see travelling like a fish
in the dawn-like quiet of the sea:
a void everywhere with us.
And the bird that flew away last winter
with a broken wing
the shelter of life,
and the young woman who left to play
with the dogteeth of summer
and the soul which screeching sought the lower world
and the country like a large plane-leaf swept along by the
    torrent of the sun
with the ancient monuments and the contemporary sorrow.

And the poet lingers, looking at the stones, and asks himself
does there really exist
among these ruined lines, edges, points, hollows, and curves
does there really exist
here where one meets the path of rain, wind, and ruin
does there exist the movement of the face, shape of the tenderness
of those who diminished so strangely in our lives,
those who remained the shadow of waves and thoughts
    boundless as the sea
or perhaps, no, nothing is left but the weight
the nostalgia of the weight of a living being
there where we now remain unsubstantial, bending
like the branches of an awful willow-tree heaped in the per-
    manence of despair
while the yellow current slowly carries down rushes uprooted
    in the mud
image of a form turned to marble by the decision of an eternal
    bitterness:
the poet a void.

Shieldbearer, the sun climbed warring,
and from the depths of the cave a startled bat
hit the light as an arrow hits a shield:
"*Ασίνην τε 'Ασίνην τε . . .*'. If only that were the King of
    Asine
we have been searching for so carefully on this acropolis
sometimes touching with our fingers his very touch upon the
    stones.

Stratis the Mariner among the Agapanthi

Transvaal, 14 January '42

There are no asphodels, no violets, no hyacinths;
how then can one talk with the dead?
The dead know the language of flowers only,
and so keep silent
they journey and are silent, endure and are silent,
beyond the community of dreams, beyond the community of
 dreams.[25]

If I start to sing I will call out
and if I call out –
the agapanthi order silence[26]
rising the tiny hand of a blue Arabian child
or even the footfalls of a goose in the air.

It is painful and difficult, the living are not enough for me
first because they do not speak, and then
because I have to ask the dead
in order to advance.
Otherwise I cannot: the moment I fall asleep
the companions cut the silver strings
and the flask of the winds empties.[27]
I fill it and it empties, I fill it and it empties;
I awaken
like a goldfish swimming
in the lightning's crevices
and the wind and the flood and the human bodies
and the agapanthi nailed like the arrows of fate
to the unquenchable earth
shaken by spasmodic nodding,

as if loaded on an ancient cart
jolting down ruined roads, over old cobblestones,
the agapanthi, asphodels of the negroes:
how can I grasp this religion?

The first thing God made is love
then comes blood
and the thirst for blood
stimulated by
the body's sperm as by salt.
The first thing God made is the long journey:
the house there is waiting
with its blue smoke
with its aged dog
waiting for the return so that it can die.
But the dead must guide me;
it is the agapanthi that hold them speechless
like the depths of the sea or the water in a glass.
And the companions remain in the palaces of Circe:
my dear Elpenor! My poor, idiotic Elpenor![28]
Or don't you see them
– 'Oh help us!' –
on the blackened ridge of Psara?[29]

An Old Man on the River Bank

Cairo, 20 June '42

And yet we must consider how we advance.
To feel is not enough, nor to think, nor to move
nor to endanger your body in an old loophole
with the scalding oil and molten lead furrow the walls.

And yet we must consider towards what we advance,
not as our pain wants it, and our hungry children
and the chasm of the companions' calling from the opposite
    shore;
nor as it is whispered by the bluish light in an improvised
    hospital,
the pharmaceutic glimmer on the pillow of the youth operated
    upon at noon;
but in some other fashion, I might wish to say as
the long river that emerges from the great lakes enclosed deep
    in Africa,
which was once a god and then became a road and a bene-
    factor, a judge and delta;
which is never the same, as the ancient wise men taught,
and yet remains always the same body, the same bed, and the
    same Sign,
the same orientation.

I want no more than to speak simply, to be granted this grace.
Because we have burdened song with so much music that it is
    gradually sinking
and we have adorned our art so much that its features have
    been eaten away by gold
and it is time to say our few words because tomorrow the soul
    sets sail.

If pain is human we are not human beings merely to suffer
    pain;
that is why I think so much these days about the great river,
this meaning which advances among herbs and greenery
and beasts that graze and drink, men who sow and harvest,
great tombs and even small habitations of the dead.
This current which goes on its way and which is not so
    different from the blood of men,
from the eyes of men when they look straight ahead without
    fear in their hearts,
without the daily tremor for trivialities or even for greater
    things;
when they look straight ahead like the traveller who is used to
    gauging his road by the stars,
not like us, the other day, gazing at the closed garden of a
    sleepy Arab house,
behind the lattices the cool garden changing shape, growing
    larger and diminishing,
we too changing, as we gazed, the shape of our desire and our
    heart,
in the drop of midday, we the patient dough of a world which
    casts us out and kneads us,
caught in the embroidered nets of a life which was complete
    and turned to dust and sank into the sands
leaving behind it only that vague dizzying sway of a tall palm-
    tree.

The Last Stop

Cava dei Tirreni, 5 October '44

Few the moonlit nights that have pleased me:
the alphabet of the stars – which you spell out
as well as your fatigue at the day's end allows
and from which you discern other meanings and other hopes –
then can be read more clearly.
Now that I sit idly and reflect,
few are the moons that remain in memory:
islands, colour of a grieving Madonna, late in the waning
or moonlight in northern cities casting sometimes
over turbulent streets, rivers, and limbs of men
a heavy torpor.
Yet here last evening, in this our final port
where we wait for the hour of our return to dawn
like an old debt, money which lay for years
in a miser's safe, and at last
the time for payment came
and coins were heard falling on the table –
in this Etruscan village, behind the sea of Salerno
behind the harbours of our return, on the edge
of an autumn squall, the moon
outstripped the clouds, and houses
on the slope opposite became enamel:
Amica silentia lunae.[30]

This is a train of thought, a way
to begin to speak of things you confess
uneasily, at times when you can't hold back, to a friend
who fled in secret and who brings
news from home and from the companions,
and you hasten to open your heart

before this exile forestalls you and alters him.
We come from Arabia, Egypt, Palestine, Syria;
the little state
of Kommagene, which flickered out like a small lamp,
often comes to mind,
and great cities which lived for thousands of years
and then became pastures for cattle,
fields for sugar-cane and corn.
We come from the sand of the desert, from the seas of Proteus,
souls shrivelled by public sins,
each holding public office, like a bird in its cage.
The rainy autumn in this cavity
infects the wound of each of us
or what you might term differently: nemesis, fate,
or simply bad habits, fraud and deceit,
or even the selfish urge to reap reward from the blood of
    others.
Man frays easily in wars;
man is soft, a sheaf of grass,
lips and fingers that hunger for a white breast
eyes that half-close in the radiance of day
and feet that would run, no matter how tired,
at the slightest call of profit.
Man is soft and thirsty like grass,
insatiable like grass, his nerves roots that stretch out;
when the harvest comes
he would rather have the scythes whistle in some other field;
when the harvest comes
some call out to exorcise the demon
some become entangled in their riches, others make orations.
But what good are exorcisms, riches, orations
when the living are far away?
Is man any different?
Is it not this which confers life:

D

a time for planting, a time for harvesting?
The same things over and over again, you will say, my friend,
But the thought of the refugee, the thought of the prisoner, the thought
of man when he too has become a commodity –
try though you may, you cannot change it.
He might even have wished to remain king of the cannibals
expending powers which no one buys,
to promenade in fields of agapanthi
to hear the drums beneath a bamboo tree,
as courtiers dance with prodigious masks.
But the country which they chop up and burn like a pine-tree, and which you see
either in the dark train, without water, the windows broken, night after night
or in the burning ship which, as the statistics indicate, will surely sink,
these things have taken root in the mind and do not change
these things have planted images like those trees
which in virgin forests cast their branches
and these take root in the earth and sprout again;
they cast their branches which sprout again, striding league after league –
and our mind a virgin forest of slain friends.
And if I speak to you in fables and parables
it is because you hear it more gently, and horror
cannot be talked about because it is alive
because it is speechless and continuous:
the memory-wounding pain
drips by day drips in sleep.[31]

To speak of heroes to speak of heroes: Michael
who fled from the hospital with open wounds
perhaps he spoke of heroes – the night

he dragged his foot through the darkened city –
when, groping, he howled out our pain: 'We advance in the
   dark,
we go forward in the dark. . . .'
The heroes go forward in the dark.

Few the moonlit nights that have pleased me.

Agianapa I [32]

And you see the light of the sun as the ancients used to say.
And yet I thought I had been seeing all these years
walking between the mountains and the sea
meeting by chance men in perfect armour;
strange, I did not notice that I saw their voices only.
It was blood that made them talk, the ram
that I slew and then spread at their feet;
but that red carpet was not the light.
Whatever they told me I had to recognize by touch
as when they hide you at night, hunted, in a stable
or when you finally reach the body of a deep-breasted woman
and the room is full of suffocating odours;
whatever they told me, skin and silk.

Strange, here I see the light of the sun; the golden net
where things quiver like fish
that a huge angel draws in
along with the nets of the fisherman.

Helen

TEUCER. .. for the sea-girt land
 of Cyprus, where Apollo prophesied that I
 should found and name New Salamis from my
 island home.
. . . .
HELEN. It was an image of me. I never went to Troy.
. . . .
SERVANT. You mean
 it was for a cloud, for nothing, we did all that work?
                                    – Euripides, *Helen*
                                    (trans. Richmond Lattimore)

'The nightingales won't let you sleep in Platres.'

Shy nightingale, in the breathing rhythm of the leaves,
you who offered music, the forest's coolness,
to the parted bodies, to the souls,
of those who know they will not return.
Blind voice, you who touch in the darkness of memory
footsteps and gestures – I wouldn't dare say kisses –
and the bitter raging of the slavewoman grown wild.

'The nightingales won't let you sleep in Platres.'

Platres: what is Platres? And this island: who knows it?
I have lived my life hearing unfamiliar names:
new countries, new idiocies of men
or of the gods;
                 my fate, which wavers
between the last sword of some Ajax
and another Salamis,
brought me here, to this shore.
                                    The moon
rose from the sea like Aphrodite,
covered the Archer's stars, now moves to find

the Heart of Scorpio, and transforms all.
Truth, where is the truth?
I too was an archer in the war;
My fate: that of a man who missed his target.

Lyric nightingale,
on a night such as this, by the shore of Proteus,
the Spartan slave girls heard you and danced their lament,
and among them – who would have thought it? – Helen!
She whom we hunted so many years by the banks of the Scamander.
She was there, at the desert's lip; I touched her; she spoke to
me:
'It isn't true, it isn't true,' she cried.
'I didn't board the blue-bowed ship.
I never went to valiant Troy.'

Deep-girdled, the sun in her hair, and that stature
shadows and smiles everywhere,
on shoulders, thighs, and knees;
the skin alive, and her eyes
with the large eyelids,
all were there, on the banks of a Delta.
                                                And at Troy?
At Troy, nothing: a phantom image.
The gods wanted it so.
And Paris, Paris lay with a shadow as though it were a solid
form.
And we slaughtered ourselves for Helen ten long years.

Great suffering had come to Greece.
So many bodies thrown
to the jaws of the sea, to the jaws of the earth
so many souls

fed to the millstones like grain.
And the rivers swelled, the blood bedded in muck,
all for a linen undulation, a bit of cloud,
a butterfly's flicker, a swan's down,
an empty tunic – all for a Helen.
And my brother?
                Nightingale nightingale nightingale,
what is a god? What is not a god. And what is the in-between
   of these?

'The nightingales won't let you sleep in Platres.'

Tearstruck bird,
               in sea-kissed Cyprus
consecrated to remind me of my country,
I moored alone with this fable,
if it is true that it is a fable,
if it is true that mortals will not again take up
the old deceit of the gods.
               If it is true
that after so many years some other Teucer,
or some Ajax or Priam or Hecuba,
or someone unknown and nameless who nevertheless saw
a Scamander overflow with corpses,
if it is true that he was not fated to hear
newsbearers coming to tell him
that so much suffering, so much life,
joined the abyss
all for an empty tunic, all for a Helen.

Pedlar from Sidon

The young pedlar came from Sidon
unafraid of angry Poseidon.
His curls crow-coloured, his chiton purple,
fastened at the shoulder by a golden clasp,
his body reeking of myrrh and make-up.
He sailed into Cyprus through Ammochoston,
now delights in the narrow sunlight
of back lanes in Nicosia.
In the courtyard a young Turkish girl:
the creeper that she trims with ivory fingers
sways shyly to her touch.
The pedlar crosses the sun's river
like a walking god, the song he sings
dream-soft: 'Roses in a kerchief . . .'
one would say his crimson lips
sought to know Zeus' sandals.
He walks on so, then stops
to sit beside a Gothic gate-post
that offers the wild-eyed lion of Mark
glaring down on a sleeping shepherd
who smells too much of goat and sweat.
The pedlar leans back; his hand
feels inside his shirt, removes
a terracotta statuette.
He studies it: a nude that glides,
uncertain, on the effeminate couch
between concave Hermes and convex Aphrodite.

Engomi [33]

Broad the plain and level; visible from a distance
the turning of arms that dug.
In the sky, the clouds all curves, here and there
a trumpet golden and rose: the sunset.
In the sparse grass and the thorns
stirred light after-shower air: it had rained
there on the peaks where the mountains took on colour.

And I moved on towards those at work,
women and men digging with picks in trenches.
It was an ancient city; walls, roads and houses
stood out like the petrified muscles of cyclopes,
the anatomy of spent strength under the eye
of the archaeologist, anaesthetist, or surgeon.
Phantasms and fabrics, luxury and lips, buried
and the curtains of pain spread wide open
to reveal, naked and indifferent, the tomb.

And I looked towards those at work,
the stretched shoulders and the arms that struck
this dead silence with a rhythm heavy and swift
as though the wheel of fate were passing through the ruins.

Suddenly I was walking and did not walk
I looked at the flying birds, and they were turned to marble
I looked at the sky's air, and it was full of wonder
I looked at the bodies that struggled, and they had stopped
and among them the light bringing forth a face.
The black hair spilled over the collar, the eyebrows
had the flutter of swallows, the nostrils
arched above the lips, and the body
emerged from the labouring hands stripped
with the unripe breasts of the Virgin,
a dance motionless.

And I lowered my eyes all round:
girls kneaded, but they did not touch the dough
women spun, but the spindles did not turn
lambs were being watered, but their tongues hung still
above green waters that seemed asleep
and the shepherd remained with his crook poised.[34]
And I looked again at that body ascending;
many had gathered, ants,
and they struck her with lances but did not wound her.
Her belly now shone like the moon
and I thought the sky was the womb
which bore her and took her back, mother and child.
Her feet remained marble still
and vanished: an Assumption.
                                      The world
became again as it had been, ours
with time and earth.
                              Aromas of mastic
began to stir on the old slopes of memory
breasts among leaves, lips moist;
and all went dry at once on the length of the plain,
in the stone's despair, in the corroded power,
in that empty place with the sparse grass and the thorns
where a snake slithered heedless
where it takes a long time to die.

ODYSSEUS ELYTIS

The Mad Pomegranate Tree

Inquisitive matinal high spirits
à perdre haleine

In these all-white courtyards where the south wind blows
Whistling through vaulted arcades, tell me, is it the mad pome-
   granate tree
That leaps in the light, scattering its fruitful laughter
With windy wilfulness and whispering, tell me, is it the mad
   pomegranate tree
That quivers with foliage newly born at dawn
Raising high its colours in a shiver of triumph?

On plains where the naked girls awake,
When they harvest clover with their light brown arms
Roaming around the borders of their dreams – tell me, is it the
   mad pomegranate tree,
Unsuspecting, that puts the lights in their verdant baskets
That floods their names with the singing of birds – tell me
Is it the mad pomegranate tree that combats the cloudy skies of
   the world?

On the day that it adorns itself in jealousy with seven kinds of
   feathers,
Girding the eternal sun with a thousand blinding prisms
Tell me, is it the mad pomegranate tree
That seizes on the run a horse's mane of a hundred lashes,
Never sad and never grumbling – tell me, is it the mad pome-
   granate tree
That cries out the new hope now dawning?
Tell me, is that the mad pomegranate tree waving in the dis-
   tance,

Fluttering a handkerchief of leaves of cool flame,
A sea near birth with a thousand ships and more,
With waves that a thousand times and more set out and go
To unscented shores – tell me, is it the mad pomegranate tree
That creaks the rigging aloft in the lucid air?

High as can be, with the blue bunch of grapes that flares and
celebrates
Arrogant, full of danger – tell me, is it the mad pomegranate
tree
That shatters with light the demon's tempests in the middle of
the world
That spreads far as can be the saffron ruffle of day
Richly embroidered with scattered songs – tell me, is it the mad
pomegranate tree
That hastily unfastens the silk apparel of day?

In petticoats of April first and cicadas of the feast of mid-
August
Tell me, that which plays, that which rages, that which can en-
tice
Shaking out of threats their evil black darkness
Spilling in the sun's embrace intoxicating birds
Tell me, that which opens its wings on the breast of things
On the breast of our deepest dreams, is that the mad pome-
granate tree?

Marina of the Rocks

You have a taste of tempest on your lips – But where did you
    wander
All day long in the hard reverie of stone and sea?
An eagle-bearing wind stripped the hills
Stripped your longing to the bone
And the pupils of your eyes received the message of chimera
Spotting memory with foam!
Where is the familiar slope of short September
On the red earth where you played, looking down
At the broad rows of the other girls
The corners where your friends left armfuls of rosemary.

But where did you wander
All night long in the hard reverie of stone and sea?
I told you to count in the naked water its luminous days
On your back to rejoice in the dawn of things
Or again to wander on yellow plains
With a clover of light on your breast, heroine of iambs.

You have a taste of tempest on your lips
and a dress red as blood
Deep in the gold of summer
And the perfume of hyacinths – But where did you wander
Descending toward the shores, the pebbled bays?

There was cold salty seaweed there
But deeper a human feeling that bled
And you opened your arms in astonishment naming it
Climbing lightly to the clearness of the depths
Where your own star-fish shone.

Listen. The word is the prudence of the aged
And time is a passionate sculptor of men
And the sun stands over it, a beast of hope
And you, closer to it, embrace a love
With a bitter taste of tempest on your lips.

It is not for you, blue to the bone, to think of another summer,
For the rivers to change their bed
And take you back to their mother
For you to kiss other cherry trees
Or ride on the north-west wind.

Propped on the rocks, without yesterday or tomorrow,
Facing the dangers of the rocks with a hurricane's hairdo
You will say farewell to the riddle that is yours.

Commemoration

I brought my life this far
To this spot which struggles
Forever near the sea
Youth upon the rocks, breast
To breast against the wind
Where is a man to go
Who is nothing other than a man
Reckoning with the coolness his green
Moments, with waters the visions
Of his hearing, with wings his remorse
O Life
Of a child who becomes a man
Forever near the sea when the sun
Teaches him to breathe there where the shadow
Of a seagull vanishes.

I brought my life this far
White addition, black total
A few trees and a few
Wet pebbles
Gentle fingers to caress a forehead
What forehead
Anticipation wept all night and is no more
Nor is anyone.
Were but a free footstep to be heard
A rested voice to rise
The poops to ripple at the jetty, inscribing
A name in darker blue upon their horizon
A few years, a few waves
Sensitive rowing
In the bays surrounding love

I brought my life this far
Bitter furrow in the sand that will vanish
– Whoever saw two eyes touch his silence
And mixed with their sunshine, closing a thousand worlds
Let him remind his blood in other suns
Nearer the light

There is a smile that pays for the flame –
But here in this ignorant landscape that loses itself
In an open and merciless sea
Success sheds
Whirling feathers
And moments that have become attached to the earth
Hard earth under the soles of impatient feet
Earth made for vertigo
A dead volcano.

I brought my life this far
A stone pledged to the liquid element
Beyond the islands
Lower than the waves
Next to the anchors
– When keels pass, splitting with passion
Some new obstacle, and triumph over it
And hope dawns with all its dolphins
The sun's gain in a human heart –
The nets of doubt draw in
A figure in salt
Carved with effort
Indifferent, white,
Which turns toward the sea the void of its eyes
Supporting infinity.

Aegean Melancholy

What linking of soul to the halcyons of the afternoon!
What calm in the voices of the distant shore!
The cuckoo in the trees' mantilla,
and the mystic hour of the fishermen's supper.
and the sea playing on its concertina
the long lament of the woman,
the lovely woman who bared her breasts
when memory found the cradles
and lilac sprinkled the sunset with fire!

With caique and the Virgin's sails
sped by the winds they are gone,
lovers of the lilies' exile;
but how night here attends on sleep
with murmuring hair on shining throats
or on the great white shores;
and how with Orion's gold sword
is scattered and spilled aloft
dust from the dreams of girls
scented with mint and basil!

At the cross-road where the ancient sorceress stood
burning the winds with dry thyme, there,
lightly, holding a pitcher full with the waters of silence,
easily, as though they were entering Paradise,
supple shadows stepped . . .
And from the crickets' prayer that fermented the fields
lovely girls with the moon's skin have risen
to dance on the midnight threshing-floor . . .

O signs, you who pass in the depths
of the mirror-holding water –
seven small lilies that sparkle –

When Orion's sword returns
it will find poor bread under the lamp
but life in the stars' embers;
it will find generous hands linked in space,
abandoned sea-weed, the shore's last children,
years, green gems . . .

O green gem – what storm-prophet saw you
halting the light at the birth of day,
the light at the birth of the two eyes of the world!

Body of Summer

A long time has passed since the last rain was heard
Above the ants and lizards
Now the sun burns endlessly
The fruit paints its mouth
The pores in the earth open slowly
And beside the water that drips in syllables
A huge plant gazes into the eye of the sun.

Who is he that lies on the shores beyond
Stretched on his back, smoking silver-burnt olive leaves?
Cicadas grow warm in his ears
Ants are at work on his chest
Lizards slide in the grass of his arm pits
And over the seaweed of his feet a wave rolls lightly
Sent by the little siren that sang:

'O body of summer, naked, burnt
Eaten away by oil and salt
Body of rock and shudder of the heart
Great ruffling wind in the osier hair
Breath of basil above the curly pubic mound
Full of stars and pine needles
Body, deep vessel of the day!

'Soft rains come, violent hail
The land passes lashed into the claws of the north wind
Which darkens in the depths with furious waves
The hills plunge into the dense udders of the clouds
And yet behind all this you laugh carefree
And find your deathless moment again
As the sun finds you again on the sandy shores
As the sky finds you again in your naked health.'

Drinking the Sun of Corinth

Drinking the sun of Corinth
Reading the marble ruins
Striding across vineyards and seas
Sighting along the harpoon
A votive fish that slips away
I found the leaves that the sun's psalm memorizes
The living land that passion joys in opening.

I drink water, cut fruit,
Thrust my hand into the wind's foliage
The lemon trees water the summer pollen
The green birds tear my dreams
I leave with a glance
A wide glance in which the world is recreated
Beautiful from the beginning to the dimensions of the heart!

This Wind that Loiters

This wind that loiters among the quinces
This bug that sucks the vines
This stone that the scorpion wears next to his skin
And these stacks on the threshing floor
That play the giant to small barefoot children.

The images of the Resurrection
On walls that the pine-trees scratched with their fingers
This whitewash that carries the noonday on its back
And the cicadas, the cicadas in the ears of the trees.

Great summer of chalk
Great summer of cork
The red sails slanting in gusts of wind
On the sea-floor white creatures, sponges
Accordions of the rocks
Perch from the fingers even of bad fishermen
Proud reefs on the fishing lines of the sun.

No one will tell our fate, and that is that.
We ourselves will tell the sun's fate, and that is that.

The Autopsy

And so they found that the gold of the olive-root had dripped
in the recesses of his heart.

And from the many times that he had lain awake by candlelight
waiting for the dawn, a strange heat had seized his entrails.

A little below the skin, the blue line of the horizon sharply
painted. And ample traces of blue throughout his blood.

The cries of birds which he had come to memorize in hours of
great loneliness apparently spilled out all at once, so that it
was impossible for the knife to enter deeply.

Probably the intention sufficed for the evil

Which he met – it is obvious – in the terrifying posture of the
innocent. His eyes open, proud, the whole forest moving
still on the unblemished retina

Nothing in the brain but a dead echo of the sky.

Only in the hollow of his left ear some light fine sand, as
though in a shell. Which means that often he had walked by
the sea alone, with the pain of love and the roar of the wind.

As for those particles of fire on his thighs, they show that he
moved time hours ahead whenever he embraced a woman.

We shall have early fruit this year.

Beauty and the Illiterate

Often, at the Dormition of Twilight,[35] her soul took on a certain lightness from the mountains opposite, though the day had been cruel and tomorrow was unknown.

Yet, when darkness came and the hand of the priest appeared over the garden of the dead, She,

Alone, Erect, with the few familiar companions of night – the rosemary breeze and the charcoal smoke from chimneys – lay awake on the threshold of the sea

Singularly beautiful.

Words half-formed of waves or half-guessed in a rustling, and others seemingly of the dead, words startled among the cypresses, like strange Zodiacs circling her head, suddenly illumined her. And an

Unbelievable clarity allowed the true landscape to appear at a great depth within her,

Where, beside the river, black men fought the Angel, showing in what manner Beauty is born.

Or what in other terms we call tears.

And as long as her thought lasted, you felt that it overflowed her shining face, with the bitterness in the eyes and the cheekbones – like those of an ancient temple-servent – enormous

Stretching from the tip of Canis Major to the tip of Virgo.

'And I, far from the pestilence of the city, imagined a desert at her side, where tears would have no meaning and where the only light would be that of the fire which devoured all my possessions

The two of us shoulder to shoulder would sustain the weight of the future, sworn to utter silence and to a condominion of the stars

As though I did not know, illiterate as I am, that it is exactly there, in utter silence, where the most appalling noises are heard

And that loneliness, from the time it became unendurable to the heart of man, has scattered and sown stars!'

NIKOS GATSOS

Amorgos

TO A GREEN STAR

'The eyes and ears are bad witnesses
for men if they have barbarian souls'
Heraclitus
(Diels, *Die Fragm. der Vorsokr.*, B. 107,
trans. Kathleen Freeman)

I.

With their country bound to the sails and their oars hung on
the wind

The shipwrecked voyagers slept tamely like dead beasts in
sheets of sponge

But the seaweeds' eyes are turned to the sea

In case the South Wind brings them back with their lateen rigs
freshly dyed,

For a single lost elephant is always worth more than the two
moving breasts of a girl,

Only in the mountains let the roofs of deserted chapels light
up at the whim of the evening star,

Let the birds flutter in the masts of the lemon tree

With the steady white beat of a new tempo;

And then the winds will come, bodies of swans that remained
spotless, tender, motionless

Among the steam-rollers of the shops, cyclones of the vege-
table gardens,

When women's eyes turned coals and the hearts of the chestnut
vendors broke,

When the harvesting stopped and the hopes of the cricket
began.

And that is why, my brave lads, with wine, kisses and leaves on
your lips,

That is why I would have you enter the rivers naked
And sing of the Barbary Coast as the woodman seeks out the
    mastic tree,
As the viper slithers through fields of barley,
Her proud eyes all anger,
As lightning threshes youth.

And don't laugh and don't weep and don't rejoice
Don't tighten your boots uselessly as though planting plane
    trees
Don't become FATED
Because the golden eagle is not a closed drawer,
Nor a plum-tree's tear, nor a water-lily's smile,
Nor a dove's vest, nor a sultan's mandolin,
Nor a silk kerchief for the head of a whale.
It is a marine saw carving gulls,
It is the carpenter's pillow, the beggar's watch,
It is fire in a smithy mocking the priests' wives and lulling the
    lilies to sleep,
It is the Turks' in-laws, the Australians' feast,
The Hungarians' mountain refuge
Where the hazel trees meet secretly in autumn:
They see the wise storks dying their eggs black
And then they too weep
They burn their nightgowns and wear the duck's petticoat
They spread stars on the ground for kings to tread on
With their silver amulets, the crown, the purple,
They scatter rosemary on garden beds
So the mice can cross to another cellar
And enter other churches to devour the sacred altars,
And the owls, my lads,
The owls are hooting
And dead nuns are rising to dance
With tambourines, drums, and violins, with bagpipes and lutes,

With banners and censers, with herbs and magic veils,
With the bear's breeches in the frozen valley,
They eat the martens' mushrooms
They play heads and tails for St John's ring and the Black
    Man's florins[36]
They ridicule the witches
They cut off a priest's beard with the cutlass of Kolokotróni[37]
They wash themselves in the smoke of incense,
And then, chanting slowly, they enter the earth again and are
    silent
As waves are silent, as the cuckoo at daybreak, as the lamplight
    at evening.

So in a deep jar the grape withers, and in the bell-tower of a fig
    tree the apple turns yellow
So, wearing a gaudy tie,
Summer breathes in the tent of a vine arbour
So, naked among the white cherry trees, sleeps my young love,
A girl unfading as an almond branch,
Her head resting on her elbow, her palm on her golden florin,
On its morning warmth, when, silent as a thief,
Through the window of spring the dawn star enters to wake
    her!

II

They say the mountains tremble and the fir-trees rage
When night gnaws the tile-pins to let in the Kallikantzari[38]
When hell gulps down the torrents' foaming toil
Or when the groomed hair of the pepper-tree becomes the
    North Wind's plaything.
Only Achaean cattle graze vigorous and strong

On abundant fields in Thessaly beneath an ageless, watching
    sun
They eat green grass and celery, leaves of the poplar tree, they
    drink clear water in the troughs
They smell the sweat of the earth and then fall heavily to sleep
    in the shade of the willow tree.

Cast out the dead said Heraclitus yet he saw the sky turn pale,
Saw two small cyclamens kissing in the mud
And as the wolf comes down from the forests to see the dog's
    carcass and weep
He too fell to kiss his own dead body on the hospitable soil.
What good to me the bead that glistens on your forehead?
I know the lightning wrote its name upon your lips
I know an eagle built its nest within your eyes
But here on this damp bank there is one way only
One deceptive way and you must take it
You must plunge into blood before time forestalls you.
Cross over opposite to find your companions again
Flowers birds deer
To find another sea, another tenderness,
To take Achilles' horses by the reins
Instead of sitting dumb scolding the river
Stoning the river like the mother of Kitso[39]
Because you too will be lost and your beauty will have aged.
I see your childhood shirt drying on the branches of a willow
Take it, this flag of life, to shroud your death
And may your heart not fail you
And may your tear not fall upon this pitiless earth
As a penguin's tear once fell in the frozen wilderness
Complaint achieves nothing
Life everywhere will be the same
With the serpent's flute in the land of phantoms

With the song of brigands in aromatic groves
With the knife of some sorrow in the cheek of hope
With the pain of some spring in the screech owl's heart –
Enough if a sharp sickle and plough are found in a joyful hand
Enough if there flowers only
A little wheat for festivals, a little wine for remembrance, a
    little water for the dust . . .

III

In the griever's courtyard no sun rises
Only worms appear to mock the stars
Only horses sprout upon the ant hills
And bats eat birds and cast off sperm.

In the griever's courtyard night never sets
Only the foliage vomits forth a river of tears
When the devil passes by to mount the dogs
And the crows swim in a well of blood.

In the griever's courtyard the eye has gone dry
The brain has frozen and the heart turned to stone
Frog-flesh hangs from the spider's teeth
Hungry locusts scream at the vampires' feet

In the griever's courtyard black grass grows
Only one night in May did a breeze pass through
A step light as a tremor on the meadow
A kiss of the foam-trimmed sea.

And should you thirst for water, we will wring a cloud

And should you hunger for bread, we will slaughter a night-
    ingale
Only wait a moment for the wild rue to open,
For the black sky to flash, the mullen to flower.

But it was a breeze that vanished, a lark that disappeared
It was the face of May, the moon's whiteness
A step light as a tremor on the meadow
A kiss of the foam-trimmed sea.

IV

Wake up limpid water from the root of the pine tree so that
you can find the sparrows' eyes and give them new life, water-
ing the earth with scent of basil and the lizard's whistling. I
know you are a naked vein under the menacing gaze of the
wind, a voiceless spark in the luminous multitude of the stars.
No one notices you, no one stops to listen to your breathing,
but you, your pace heavy in the arrogant ranks of nature, will
one day reach the leaves of the apricot tree, will one day
climb the slender bodies of young broom shrubs, will fall from
the eyes of a beloved one like an adolescent moon. There is a
deathless stone on which a passing human angel once inscribed
his name and a song that no one yet knows, not even the
craziest children or the wisest nightingales. It is now locked up
in a cave of Mount Devi, in the gorges and ravines of my
fatherland, but someday when it breaks out and thrusts itself
against destruction and time, this angelic song, the rain will
suddenly stop and the mud dry up, the snows will melt in the
mountains, the wind will sing like a bird, the swallows will
come to life, the willows will shiver, and the men of cold eyes
and pallid faces – when they hear the bells tolling of their own
accord in the cracked belltowers – will find festive hats to wear
and gaudy bows to decorate their shoes. Because then no one

will joke any longer, the blood of the brooks will overflow, the animals will break their bridles in the mangers, the hay will turn green in the stables, between the roof-tiles fresh poppies will sprout, and May flowers, and at all crossroads red fires will rise at midnight. Then slowly the frightened young girls will come to cast their last clothing into the fire and dance all naked around it, just as in our day, when we too were young, and a window would open at dawn to show a flaming carnation growing on their breasts. Lads, maybe the memory of ancestors is deeper consolation and more precious company than a handful of rose water, and the intoxication of beauty no different from the sleeping rose bush of the Eurotas. So now goodnight; I see a galaxy of falling stars rocking your dreams, but I hold in my fingers music for a better day. Travellers from India have more to tell you than the Byzantine chroniclers.

V

Man, during the course of this mysterious life,
Bequeathed his descendants tokens varied and worthy of his immortal origin,
As he bequeathed also traces of the ruins of twilight, snow-drifts of celestial reptiles, diamonds, kites, and the glances of hyacinths,
In the midst of sighs, tears, hunger, wailing, and the ashes of subterranean wells.

VI

How very much I loved you only I know
I who once touched you with the eyes of the Pleiades,
Embraced you with the moon's mane, and we danced on the meadows of summer
On the harvest's stubble and together ate cut clover,
Great dark sea with so many pebbles round your neck, so many coloured jewels in your hair.

A ship nears shore, a rusted water-wheel groans.
A tuft of blue smoke in the rose of the horizon
Is like a crane's wing palpitating.
Armies of swallows are waiting to offer the brave their welcome
Arms rise naked, anchors engraved on the armpits
Children's cries mingle with the song of the West Wind
Bees come and go in the cows' nostrils
Kalamata[40] kerchiefs flutter
And a distant bell painting the sky with bluing
Is like the sound of a gong travelling among the stars –
A gong that escaped so many ages ago
From the souls of Goths and the domes of Baltimore[41]
And from lost Saint Sophia, the great cathedral.

But up in the high mountains who are they who now gaze
down, eyes calm, faces serene?
Of what conflagration is this cloud of dust the echo?
Is Kalyvas[42] fighting now, or is it Leventoyannis[43]
Have the Germans begun to battle the noble men of Mani?[44]
Kalyvas isn't fighting, nor is Leventoyannis
Nor have the Germans begun to battle the noble men of
Mani.
Silent towers guard a ghostly princess
The tips of cypress trees consort with a dead anemone
Shepherds unperturbed pipe their morning song on a linden
reed
A stupid hunter fires a shot at the turtledoves
And an old windmill, forgotten by all,
Mends by himself his rotten sails with a needle of dolphin bone
And descends the slopes with a brisk northwester leading him
As Adonis descended the paths of Mt Chelmos to bid the love-
sick shepherdess[45] good evening.

For years and years, O my tormented heart, have I struggled
    with ink and hammer,
With gold and fire, to fashion an embroidery for you,
The hyacinth of an orange tree,
A flowering quince tree to comfort you –
I who once touched you with the eyes of the Pleiades,
Embraced you with the moon's mane, and we danced on the
    meadows of summer
On the harvest's stubble and together ate cut clover
Great dark loneliness with so many pebbles round your neck,
    so many coloured jewels in your hair.

Death and the Knight (*1513*)[46]

As I behold you motionless
journeying through the ages with the steed of Acritas and the
    lance of Saint George,[47]
I could place near you,
with these dark forms that will assist you always,
until one day you too will vanish with them forever,
until you become a fire again in the great womb of Fate that
    gave you birth,
I could place near you
a bitter orange-tree in the snow-covered meadows of the
    moon,
could unfold before you the veil of some evening,
with the red star of Scorpio singing of youth
with the River of Heaven spilling into August
with the North Star weeping and freezing,
I could place pastures,
streams that once watered the lilies of Germany,
and this armour that you wear, I could adorn it
with a basil-shoot and a spray of mint
with the weapons of Plapoutas and Nikitaras' trophies.[48]
But I who saw your descendants like birds
tear the sky of my country one spring dawn,
saw the cypresses of Morea hush
there on the plain of Nauplia,
before the ready embrace of the wounded sea,
where the centuries have fought with the crosses of courage,
I will now place near you
the embittered eyes of a child,
the closed eyelids
in the mud and blood of Holland.

This black land
will grow green some day.
The iron hand of Goetz will overturn the carts,[49]
will load them with sheaves of barley and rye,
and in the dark forests with their dead loves,
there where time turned a virgin leaf to stone,
on breasts where a tearful rose trembled lightly,
a silent star will shine like a spring daisy.

But you will stay motionless;
with the steed of Acritas and the lance of St George
you will journey through the ages,
a restless hunter from the generation of heroes,
with these dark forms that will assist you always,
until one day you too will vanish with them forever,
until you become a fire again in the great womb of Fate that
    gave you birth,
until again in the river caves resound
heavy hammers of patience
not for rings and swords[50]
but for pruning-knives and ploughs.

Notes

(For fuller notes to most of the poems in this anthology, as well as for critical commentary on the poets included, readers are referred to the translators' *Six Poets of Modern Greece*, London, 1960.)

I. BIOGRAPHICAL NOTES

1. Constantine P. Cavafy (Kavafis) was born in Alexandria, Egypt, in 1863. Of Constantinopolitan descent, he spent the greater part of his childhood in England, and knew English fluently. For most of his life he was employed as a civil servant in the Egyptian Ministry of Public Works. He died in Alexandria in 1933.

2. George Seferis (pen-name of Seferiadis) was born in Smyrna in 1900. He moved with his family to Athens in 1914, studied in Paris from 1918 to 1924, and in 1926 joined the Greek Diplomatic Service. During World War II he served with the Free Greek Government in Crete, S. Africa, Egypt, London and Italy. From 1957 to 1962 he was Greek Ambassador in London, and in 1963 he was awarded the Nobel Prize for literature. He now lives in Athens.

3. Odysseus Elytis (pen-name of Alepoudelis) was born in Crete in 1911 of a well-known industrial family. He studied Law and Political Science at the University of Athens, and Philology in Paris. He has spent several years in France, and in 1961 visited the United States. He lives in Athens.

4. Nikos Gatsos was born in Arcadia in 1914, and studied Philology at the University of Athens. Besides writing his own poetry, he has made a number of translations, in particular of the plays and poems of Lorca. He lives in Athens.

II. NOTES ON THE TEXT:

1. cf. Plutarch, *Life of Antony*, par. 75, and Shakespeare, *Antony and Cleopatra*, IV, iii.

2. See Edwyn Bevan, *The House of Seleucus* (London,1902), Vol. II, p. 159.

3. Plutarch, in his *Life of Pompey*, says that Theodotus of Chios persuaded the Egyptians to kill Pompey when he landed.

4. Manuel Comnenos was Byzantine Emperor, 1143–80.

5. In the spring of A.D. 68, Galba, then in Spain, was invited to replace Nero; on the latter's suicide in the same year, he took the title of Caesar and went to Rome.

6. Demetrius Soter was one of the grandchildren of Antiochus the Great, the King of Syria, who had lost his kingdom to the Romans at the Battle of Magnesia in 190 B.C. Demetrius Soter was sent to Rome as a hostage, but on the death of Antiochus he asked to be set free. The Senate refused, and so he escaped secretly. He returned to Syria, the people declared in his favour, and finally he obtained recognition as king from the Romans. He expelled the satrap Heracleides from Babylon, thus earning the title Soter. But through the excesses of his life he lost his people's support, was overthrown by an impostor, Balas, and killed by him in battle.

7. Mithridates VI, Eupator Dionysus (the 'Great') was the last of a line of kings of the Pontus of the same name.

8. Botaneiatis is the Byzantine Emperor Nikephoros III Botaneiatis, dethroned in 1081 by Alexios I Comnenos, whose wife was the Irene Doukaina mentioned here.

9. The philosopher Ammonius (d. A.D. 243; 'Sakkas' because he had been a sack-carrier) taught at Alexandria and is supposed to have had both Plotinus and Origen among his pupils.

10. The quotation heading this poem is from a satirical work of the Emperor Julian the Apostate in which he upbraids

the people of Antioch, then a Christian city, for their hostile attitude towards his attempts to restore his prudish and moralistic form of paganism. The poem is the response of the Antiochians to Julian's pedantic reproof.

11. In 363 the Emperor Julian was killed and Jovian, a Christian, was elected in his stead. Jovian's support of orthodoxy made him, for the Christians, a welcome successor to Julian (in Syrian literature he even became the subject of a Christian romance), and the poem expresses the relief of the Antiochians at the change. See also *Julian and the Antiochians*.

12. Kleomenes (King of Sparta 236–222 B.C.) had agreed to send his mother, Kratesiclea, and his children as hostages to Egypt on the condition that Ptolemy III Euergetes, King of Egypt, would send him aid in his war against Macedonia and the Achaean League. (See Plutarch's *Life of Agis and Kleomenes*.)

13. Zabinas, Grypos, and Hyrcanus are in fact historical personages, but from the point of view of the poem it is not important to know more about them than the text makes clear: that they had rival interests in the throne of Syria.

14. See notes to *Julian and the Antiochians* and *A Great Procession of Priests and Laymen*.

15. *Mythical Story* is a group of twenty-four closely related poems, with a central *persona*. The literal meaning of the title is 'novel', but it has other connotations, as the poet indicates in the following note:

MYTHICAL STORY – it is its two components that made me choose the title of this work: 'myth', because I have used, clearly enough, a certain mythology; 'story', because I have tried to express, in a certain sequence, a state of mind as independent of me as are the characters in a novel.

The title is followed by an epigraph from Rimbaud: 'Si j'ai du goût, ce n'est guère Que pour la terre et les pierres.'

16. The quotation is from Plato, *Alcibiades*, 133 B.

17. See Homer, Od. xi. 75 ff.

18. See Od. xi.

19. The Symplegades, through which Jason and the Argonauts had to pass, were dangerous clashing rocks at the juncture of the Bosphorus and the Pontus Euxinus, or Black Sea.

20. See Od. x. 552 ff.

21. See Od. xi.

22. See Od. x. 526.

23. 'Santorini is geologically composed of pumice-stone and china-clay; in her bay, islands have appeared and disappeared. This island was once the birthplace of a very ancient religion. The lyrical dance of a strict and heavy rhythm performed here was called: *Gymnopaedia*.' – Guide to Greece.

24. i.e., the ruined citadel of Asine on a bluff near Nauplia.

25. See Od. xxiv. 12 ff.

26. Agapanthi are African lilies.

27. See Od. x.

28. Elpenor, to whom reference has been made in *Mythical Story* (e.g. Nos. 4 and 12), is a central figure in Seferis's myth.

29. This line is from Solomos's *The Destruction of Psara*, (1825). The island of Psara was razed and its people massacred during the Greek War of Independence.

30. See Virgil, *Aeneid*, ii, 255.

31. See Aeschylus, *Agamemnon*, 179–80.

32. Agianapa (sometimes spelled Ayia Napa) is a village near the sea to the south of Famagusta, Cyprus.

33. Engomi is a village to the north west of Famagusta, Cyprus.

34. Compare lines 21–37 of this poem to the passage relating to the Virgin's birth of Christ in 'The Book of James, or Protevangelium', XVIII, 2, of *The Apocryphal New Testament*.

35. The allusion is to the Dormition of the Virgin.

36. The Black Man is the 'Arapis' of Greek folk literature, who emerges at night to feed his flocks with gold pieces.

37. Kolokotróni: Theodoros Kolokotrónis, 1770–1843 was one of the principal heroes of the Greek War of Independence (1821–8).

38. 'Kallikantzari' are gross, bestial, destructive creatures who appear at night during the twelve days after Christmas.

39. Kitso was a Greek chieftain who fought against the Turks. He was captured and was about to be hanged when his mother tried to join him from the opposite bank of an impassable river. In a popular ballad she is pictured as rebuking the river, throwing stones at it and pleading with it to let her cross over to her son.

40. Kalamáta is a town in the southern Peloponnesus, noted for its olives and for its multicoloured silk kerchiefs.

41. Baltimore: an allusion to Edgar Allan Poe's 'The Bells'.

42. Kalyvas and Leventoyannis were both heroes of the Greek War of Independence, in which both were killed.

44. Mani is the rocky south of the Peloponnesus, legendary because the Turks were unable to occupy it on account of the bravery of its inhabitants.

45. Shepherdess: the shepherdess referred to is Golfo, the heroine of a nineteenth century play of small dramatic merit though still popular, written by Spiridon Peresiadis. Golfo lives in a village on Mount Chelmos near Patras; she is driven mad by the loss of her lover.

46. The title and some of the imagery of this poem were suggested by Durer's famous copperplate engraving, 'The Knight, Death, and the Devil' (1513).

47. Acritas is the warrior hero of the Byzantine epic, *Digenis Acritas*.

48. Plapoutas and Nikitaras, heroes of the Greek War of Independence, were renowned for feats of great individual courage.

49. Goetz von Berlichingen (1480–1562) was a German knight whose right arm was shot away in 1505 while he was assisting Albert IV, Duke of Bavaria, at the siege of Landshut; he substituted an iron arm and became known as 'Goetz with the iron hand'. Goethe made him the hero of his play, '*Götz von Berlichingen*' (1771).

50. The allusion is to Wagner's *Der Ring des Nibelungen*.

More about Penguins

If you have enjoyed reading this book you may wish to know that *Penguin Book News* appears every month. It is an attractively illustrated magazine containing a complete list of books published by Penguins and still in print, together with details of the month's new books. A specimen copy will be sent free on request.

Penguin Book News is obtainable from most bookshops; but you may prefer to become a regular subscriber at 3s. for twelve issues. Just write to Dept EP, Penguin Books Ltd, Harmondsworth, Middlesex, enclosing a cheque or postal order, and you will be put on the mailing list.

Two new reference books published by Penguins are described overleaf.

Note: *Penguin Book News* is not
available in the U.S.A.

Two important new Penguin reference books

THE PENGUIN ENGLISH DICTIONARY

Containing more than 45,000 entries and specially prepared for Penguins by a team led by Professor G. N. Garmonsway of London University, this new dictionary places particular emphasis on current usage. Definitions, which include hundreds of post-war words and senses, are as direct and simple as possible, and a new and immediately understandable system is introduced as a guide to pronunciation. In all *The Penguin English Dictionary* makes an unrivalled catalogue of English words as used today in print and speech.

THE PENGUIN ENCYCLOPEDIA

This concise and authoritative new encyclopedia has been geared deliberately for use in the second half of the twentieth century. Articles by specialists, under more than 6,000 main headings, pay particular attention to the rapidly advancing areas of science and technology; but the arts and humanities have not been neglected. These simple, accurate and intelligent explanations are likely to prove equally handy for the schoolboy, the student and the family bookshelf. Specially commissioned for Penguins, this up-to-date work is remarkably comprehensive and fully cross-referenced. It will be followed by a gazetteer and a dictionary of biography.